ARMY GIRL

The Untold Story

Pauline Cole

Copyright © Pauline Cole 2015
This book is sold subject to the condition that it shall not, by way of trade or otherwise, be lent, resold, hired out, or otherwise circulated without the publisher's prior consent in any form of binding or cover other than that in which it is published and without a similar condition including this condition being imposed on the subsequent publisher.
The moral right of Pauline Cole has been asserted.
ISBN-13: 978-1522837251
ISBN-10: 1522837256

CONTENTS

Introduction *1*
Chapter One *5*
Chapter Two *15*
Chapter Three *29*
Chapter Four *40*
Chapter Five *45*
Chapter Six *58*
Chapter Seven *76*
Aden: the political background 1838 – 2015 .... *84*

INTRODUCTION

This summer, 2015, Pauline Cole will attend the Buckingham Palace Garden Party under the auspices of Blind Veterans, UK. She remains the only blind ex-servicewoman in the country, a veteran of one of the nastiest fields of action since the Second World War. Although trained in communications, Pauline found herself in the front line during the Aden Emergency, 1967. She saw active service, used weapons in danger and coped at first hand with Arab and Egyptian terrorists. After Aden, her army career took her to Germany where she manned the telephone exchange during a crucial period of the Cold War. Civil life found her running everything she ever started, whether it was the local Co-op, a nightclub, charity ventures for children, or her own business mailing leisure catalogues.

Now retired, Pauline lives near her two adult sons and their families in Eastbourne, East Sussex. Her experiences in Aden remain the highlight of her life and she has begun research into the political background of a campaign that she saw on the ground, never feeling entirely confident that the Government took proper steps to safeguard their moral responsibility towards a former Crown Colony.

She is a vocal spokesman for the virtues of Army training. The disciplines served her well throughout her life: she loved the camaraderie, the physical demands and even the dangers involved. It might not suit every young woman – but Pauline was a very round peg in a very round hole.

Pauline at work on a manual switchboard: it needed a cool head as well as technical skill. She became a pin up girl for the local newspapers.

"There was fun to be had outside the camp as well. The Marquis of Bath needed some extra manpower for his Wildlife Safari Park at Longleat. Could the Commandant at Tidworth spare a handful of soldiers for an occasional weekend? Loads of people put their hands up and I was very lucky to be picked. We got paid, but the excitement was worth far more. It was a wonderful opportunity to drive around the estate and see the animals. Lions roaming around in relatively natural surroundings were a rare sight in England then, and the idea of a safari park in a stately home was relatively new. The visitors seemed to be mostly Americans.

"I passed my training and I was sent to Aldershot. When you go to another camp, you've got to learn the extensions all over again, and they've got to be in your head in a fortnight. At least the Aldershot Exchange only had a six position board: we'd had eighteen at Salisbury. I didn't like Aldershot. It was a huge, rough Army base and the entire town seemed to be populated by Army wives and children. I put in for an overseas posting. I wanted to see the world."

From Pauline's scrap book:
Aden posting, November 1966.

"One day, I was summoned by a senior officer. 'Private Cole,' she said, 'you've got an overseas posting.'

'Brilliant. Ma'am,' I told her. 'Where?' She told me that I was to be sent to Aden. Apparently, senior command thought I could handle active service. At that stage, I was only a Private, but my new appointment required me to have a rank and I was promoted to Lance-Corporal. I didn't know much about Aden then, but I was told that only a few women accepted posts to the Middle East and generally they worked in wages and administration. I must expect not to be able to go home on leave very often as the distance was too great.

"At home, everyone in John Dickinson knew that my Dad's daughter was going to Aden on active service to fight for Britain! Dad was incredibly proud of me – all my mother did was cry. She said, 'You can't go out there, it's on television, soldiers are being killed.'

I said, 'I'm going.'

"I wasn't leaving anyone special behind. I had lots of boy friends, but no boyfriend. It was considered really bad to become pregnant when you weren't married. Single mothers were not acceptable in those days and society frowned upon you, especially if you had been training for a career outside the home. Pregnant women were sent away to an 'aunt' and the babies were adopted. It had happened to a few of my friends and I really didn't want to risk the possibility. I wouldn't have been able to stay in the Army. So I became good friends with the young men I knew, and I made it perfectly clear that nothing else was on the cards.

"Aden? I knew where it was, and that was probably the extent of my knowledge. Today, I would google it and have the relevant facts in seconds. In those days, all I could do was climb onto the aeroplane at Gatwick and head off into the greatest adventure of my life."

Aden from the air. Peaceful from 30,000 feet up.

CHAPTER ONE

Aden lies on the east of a vast natural harbour in the Gulf of Aden and guards the entrance to the Red Sea. In ancient days, part of the harbour occupied the crater of a dormant volcano and the original port city is still called Crater. It was connected to the mainland by a narrow isthmus which forms a harbour and port to the west. This volcanic peninsula became known as Little Aden, crucially important in modern times as an oil refinery and tanker port.

The point of Aden was always its geographical location. Lying between India and Europe, and almost precisely equidistant from Suez Canal, Bombay and Zanzibar, it became one of the busiest ports in the world, as well as one of the most culturally significant: cities such as Mecca could only be supplied by ships through Aden. Historically, it was a very desirable possession and fought over since ancient times. In 1838, it was acquired by the British East India Company, who landed Royal Marines at Aden to secure the territory and stop attacks by pirates against British shipping. Aden was governed as part of British India and known as the Aden Settlement until it was detached from India to become a Crown Colony in 1937.

After the Suez crises in 1956, Aden became the main location in the region for the British who had two ambitions: to secure trading interests and to stabilise the surrounding area in preparation for eventual independence. But compared to other former British Empire possessions, development towards self-government and local participation in Aden was painfully slow. Sharia law was never used.

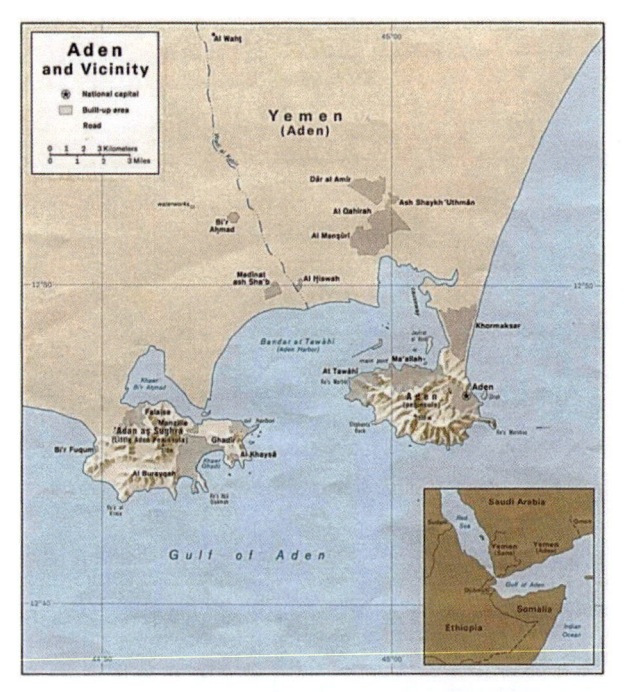

Historical map of British India showing Aden in the 1890s.

Until 1955, the three local government bodies were kept under control of an unelected Executive Council responsible to a British Governor and judicial administration was secular and British.

English king, Aden stamp.

In 1959, a Chief Minister of Aden was democratically elected on a constitutional basis of universal suffrage. He disliked the idea of Aden belonging to a South Arabian Federation and, in consequence, was dismissed and sent into exile.

In 1963, the Aden Colony was incorporated into a Federation of Arab Emirates of the South and renamed The State of Aden. The Federation would include disparate states of the region, including the Egyptian Republicans of North Yemen. The following year, Britain announced that it would work towards establishing independence to the Federation of Arab States but that the British military would remain in Aden to provide stability and confidence. In effect, we were assisting the Federal Army against dissidents from the Yemen.

Almost immediately, military rebels in the Yemen overthrew the Imam, proclaimed the birth of a Yemen Arab Republic and begged for help from Egypt. Within weeks, tens of thousands of Egyptian troops arrived and both the Yemen and Egypt were plunged into a multi-sided civil war. In the Yemen itself, Egyptians and Republicans, with Russian and Chinese support, were locked in battle with supporters from the old Imamate, in turn backed by arms and money from the Saudis who proclaimed a holy war against Communists and supporters of Nasser on the sacred soil of Arabia. The new South Arabia Federation became an uneasy alliance on the shifting sands of Middle Eastern politics.

Britain was almost as divided as the new Federation. Traditionally, Conservative Policy had been to maintain Protectorates, understanding and accepting an Imperial responsibility. Inevitably, Labour felt that the Empire was an embarrassing feudal remnant to be got rid of, as fast as decently possible. The Labour Government's plan to 'abandon' Aden was not just political contrivance or a deliberate calculation of material costs, but a genuine belief that continued maintenance of the base was hindering a rapprochement with local nationalists – yet they never sought the opinion of the local nationalists involved. Tricky questions of sovereignty were dodged and ducked. There were eighty thousand 'British Nationals' in Aden; what would happen to them? In law, they would become citizens of the new Arab state – but what if they didn't want to?

Steamer Point, Aden.

In 1963, an insurgency against the British administration began with a grenade attack from the Communist National Liberation Front which killed one person and injured fifty. A state of emergency was declared. In his book 'Having Been a Soldier', Colonel Mitchell declared that if we (the British) had been strong and determined enough to defeat the first subversive elements, we would have saved hundreds of lives and stabilised the entire area including the Persian Gulf. He knew the Russians wanted Aden as a base, an ambition fostered by the Communist NLF. He also knew that the Arabs respected a show of strength: indeed that it was something expected from a powerful and educated military presence.

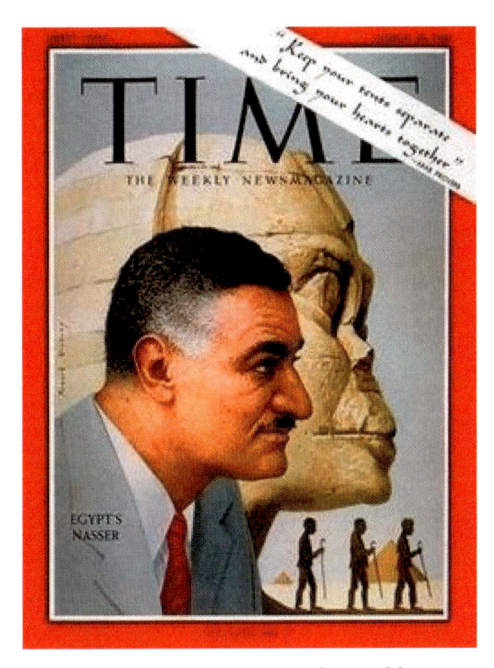

Coverman: Nasser on the world stage.

In June 1967, an event occurred which was to change the political background dramatically in the Middle East. Gamel Abdul Nasser, who had somehow established himself as an Arab leader against Israel, over-reached himself. He had, with Russian help, built up an impressive army and air force. He decided to block the Gulf of Aqaba, a vital Israeli shipping route.

The Israelis took this as an act of war. Already mobilised for an expected campaign, they took the initiative and virtually destroyed the Egyptian air force on the ground. Then they occupied the Gaza Strip and pushed into Sinai, destroying Egyptian armour and driving the Egyptians before them like sheep. To drive their point home, they threw the surprised Jordanians out of Jerusalem and advanced into Syria. There, they occupied the Golan Heights. The war lasted exactly six days. The blow to Arab prestige in general and

Nasser in particular was enormous. One-eyed General Dayan was asked how it was possible to win a war in six days. He was reported to have replied 'arrange to fight the Arabs'.

His defeat was too late to hinder the growth of the National Liberation Front who had already acquired sufficient armaments and influence to become a major threat in Aden. In 1967, there were mass riots between the NLF and FLOSY (Front for the Liberation of Occupied South Yemen) despite the intervention of British troops. No one seems to have asked the Arabs if they wanted independence. They fought each other and they fought against the British. Mitchell, a lone voice, seems to have understood what his political masters never did: that the base depended upon local goodwill to survive. Essentially, the Arab states were pro-British but if communist factions grew too powerful, the base would need a greater military presence to defend itself. Its very existence produced a bigger problem than the one it was designed to protect. Colonel Mitchell wrote that 'military sense is entitled to prevail over political policy if the latter is obviously unrealistic and bound to lead to disaster'.

That belief defined the gallant soldier – and was to lead to his ultimate downfall.

Pauline was indeed going to a war zone, in more senses than one.

Crater, old town in the volcano crater.

"Our flight out was in a bumpy old aeroplane which stopped at Bahrain to refuel. There were no stewardesses, and no frills – men only and hard seats. Aden had one runway and the aeroplane just stopped before it ran out into the sand. The first thing that hit you was the heat. It made you gasp, and take a breath. A Land Rover with a metal top met us at the airport. It was driven by a soldier with a gun and an armed guard. Our base was Steamer Point, a twenty minute drive along what became known as 'Murder Mile', a stretch of road with a concrete wall down the centre which meant traffic had to go up and down, presenting a far easier target for snipers. I was dying for a shower. First, I met the Duty Officer and the girls in my camp. They asked me if I liked cockroaches? This wasn't an idle question. Cockroaches were the bane of the base. They were the size of your thumb and they flew. They were fairly harmless but they were everywhere and they particularly liked water. My colleagues got rid of the current occupants of the shower for me, and ran the water. It was a tradition, for new recruits, and I did the same, in my turn. Crunch, crunch.

"I went to the Quartermaster's Store to be fitted for my army dress, knee length and sleeves just above the elbow. We wore Jesus sands and a beret, worn sideways. Us girls were all given £30 to buy cotton underwear, easier in the heat than nylon for bras and knickers. Eight o'clock the following morning, a Land Rover came to collect me for work. Steamer Point was a big base at the foot of a mountain with a private beach, fenced off by land and under water from the Arabs. The switchboard lay halfway up the mountain and the hospital was at the top. The two position board was operated by two girls and guarded by soldiers. One operator would plug in and the other would listen and take notes, if necessary. I watched and learnt: I certainly began to know what was going on.

Pauline in new uniform dress, sandals and beret in Aden.

"The telephone lines were laid in the sand and covered up as much as possible. If the Arabs found them, they'd blow them up and we would lose all connection with the airport – and everyone else. Linesmen would go out with a ferret (small tank) and large gun to repair them. Our shifts on the board were quite easy, depending on what was going on. The sound of grenades and bombs going off all the time became normal.

"After a week, we were taken to Khormakasar for arms training. We were shown how to use machine guns with reels of bullets, automatic rifles with magazines and a pistol. Why a pistol, I'll never know. If you run out of machine guns and rifles and there's a hundred Arabs running towards you, there isn't much you can do with a pistol except turn it on yourself. Given the nature of the Arabs, that would probably be your best bet. I was a good shot with a pistol, and not bad with the machine gun and the rifle.

"We were taught how to dismantle arms and reassemble them – I broke all my nails! It was hard work, they were heavy. Men fired machine guns from their shoulders: we had to fire from the hip because the recoil was strong enough to break our collar bones. It was less likely to damage our hips, although I got some cracking bruises.

"In the second week, we were taught basic first aid. It wasn't medical training, but knowing how to stop a bleed and apply a tourniquet might save a life. The men enjoyed practising on us! The third week was when we learnt self-defence – how to throw someone over your shoulder or trip them up. I couldn't really see the point of this, I wasn't going to wrestle with an Arab. If that situation arose, the important point was to get them down on the ground."

There were forty Army women on the Aden base and fifty-five thousand men. Pauline doesn't think she ever bought a drink. "There weren't any problems, at least not as far as I knew. The men loved women's company and they missed their families. It was like brothers and sisters: it was the army camaraderie. If a bunch of us girls were spotted in the NAAFI or on the beach, the squaddies fought to offer us a Coca-Cola. Bees round a honeypot. We used to meet in the evening at 'The Exclusive Club' which did double duty as a fire station in the day."

But it wasn't all high jinks and beach parties, terrorism – assassination, grenade throwing and sabotage – was increasing as gunmen systematically wiped out the Special Branch officers of the Aden police and blinded the security services.

Officialdom seemed powerless, believing that tough measures would alienate the local population. There was, apparently, no deterrent to the terrorists who were rarely caught and never executed: captured terrorists were placed in a detention centre, to be released as 'heroes' in eighteen months. Their only danger was the risk of being shot by an alert soldier or sentry whilst carrying out seditious acts. In January 1967, there were mass riots between the NLF and their rival FLOSY supporters in the old Arab quarter of Aden, despite the intervention of British troops. Increasing violence threatened the British Government's plans for a peaceful withdrawal as well as compromising plans for simultaneous independence.

CHAPTER TWO

Colin Mitchell had been a soldier since the age of fifteen when he enlisted with the Home Guard in 1940. He was commissioned into the Argylls in 1944 and saw active service in Italy where he was lightly wounded. After the war, he served in Palestine for three years. He was shot by mistake and after recovering from his injuries, he was appointed Aide-de-camp to General Gordon MacMillan, Commander of British forces in Palestine and Transjordan. He made friends with Arabs and Jews, and became close to Moshe Dayan, a friendship that would be life-long.

In 1950, he rejoined his regiment and deployed to Korea for dangerous manoeuvres against the Chinese communists: this was followed by service in Cyprus against EOKA terrorists. Mitchell was subsequently posted to East Africa with his regiment and the King's African Rifles where they helped break up disturbances between Arabs and Africans in Zanzibar. Following service in Kenya, Mitchell was dispatched to Borneo and six months of jungle warfare during the Indonesian-Malaysian confrontation.

Colin Mitchell was earning a reputation as a bold and efficient soldier. He was a short, handsome man with a direct, pugnacious manner who spoke robust, unminced language that had not been used by Army officers since the decline of the British Empire. His men thought the world of him – his Government were to think a good deal less, a situation which was entirely mutual.

Meanwhile, Pauline and her colleagues were attempting to keep the lid on Aden. "Twice a week, we would go out on checkpoint duty. Senior officers would decide where the checkpoint would be situated.

Picturesque uniforms conceal a fighting spirit second to none: the Argylls.

Colonel Mitchell: somehow, a news cameraman was always on hand to record him in action which infuriated Whitehall.

"A three tonner took thirty men and two Land Rovers carried us girls to the temporary wooden structure which was built like a bridge to stop and check the traffic. A car would bump along the sand towards us and it was like the old woman who lived in a shoe. Out would come a goat, a dog, three children, two men, a bird and I don't know what else. I was always amazed what the Arabs squashed into one car. My job was to take the Arab women behind a screen to search them. Although we were taught to respect their culture, we had to make certain that they weren't hiding anything under their black garments that could be used to make a bomb.

"Mostly, their hair was up in a bun and we had to poke our fingers carefully through it: I'm afraid to say that they were foul, greasy and they smelled. They covered their hands and arms with henna and I've no idea if they ever washed. We had to search every bit of them – they never used sanitary towels.

Anything could be hidden under their national dress.

"Sometimes, they objected and raised their hands to hit you – we'd step back. We were having lessons in Arabic and soon learnt a few words. Some came from a different tribe.

One lot were over six foot tall and carried a rod to keep them upright. We hated them and they hated us. If we got a tall one, we had to watch out. They hit."

Pauline was tested to the limit more than once. All baskets had to be emptied and the contents laid out on the sand. Sometimes the women refused. Politeness didn't always work. Pauline had to demonstrate the authority of her position. She had to shout: she had to meet dumb insolence and point-blank refusal with determined strength. One woman had a flask in her basket. 'Open it,' Pauline commanded.

'You open it,' came the reply.

'No. YOU open it.' Eventually, staring at her, the Arab tipped the harmless stew out onto the sand.

'Mind games,' said Pauline, but it was a tense situation that threatened to get out of hand at any moment. They weren't playing cowboys and Indians – they were at war. This was real.

Wessex, beach landing, Aden.

A certain historical ambiguity existed in Anglo-Arab relationships. Although Aden had been part of the British Empire since 1838, the first acquisition for a new young

Queen Victoria, the Indian Political Service relinquished control of Aden in 1917. In 1937 its 'protectorate' status meant that defence and external affairs continued to be handled by the British, whilst a new treaty with neighbourhood tribesmen, 'Ingram's Peace,' allowed the English to become involved in Arabian internal affairs. Aden became a 'Crown Colony', a transition from vice regal Indian administration's influence to Whitehall although an English judicial system had always been the rule. But whilst Indian officials were increasingly preoccupied by their own independence struggles in the mid-1940s, post-war England had little time to worry about outposts of the Empire.

Aden began to flourish with the Indian shopkeepers and Arab landlords of Steamer Point who gladly joined forces with the Treaty Sheikhs of the wider Protectorate to secure the British base – and British patronage – indefinitely. But the same wealth encouraged an influx of Arab workers who made a natural seedbed for anti-British revolution. In September 1962, the Colonial Government passed a Bill to unite the Crown Colony and surrounding Protectorate in the mutually protective Federation of South Arabia. But – British administrators ignored the increasing rancour of the workers. They had copied British Trade Unions and learnt how to strike: we never quite learned how to stop them, either in Docklands or Aden.

As Aden struggled towards a largely reluctant independence in 1967, did any noble Lord or Honourable Member arguing in Westminster that year remember that we had first promised to support the creation of an independent Arab state in 1917 in exchange for Arab support in the First World War? That the British encouraged an Arab revolt against the Ottoman-Turkish Empire who were attacking Aden? And that Lawrence of Arabia accompanied Prince Feisal to the Peace Conference in Versailles to discuss it? Lawrence, reminiscent of Colin Mitchell, was short, charismatic and heroic.

If the British Government fluffed and obfuscated, men like Lawrence and Mitchell stand out as soldiers of integrity. Neither were easily assimilated into their milieu: neither ever earned the rewards handed out to lesser men. Britain encourages eccentric heroes up to a point: eventually, they need to play the game to be accepted by the Establishment. All institutions require team players. Individuals are difficult. Lawrence and Mitchell were never going to fit in.

The real Lawrence of Arabia: a story almost too dramatic to be true.

Everyone tried to overlook the picturesque Arab costumes that 'Al Auruns' sported in the Hall of Mirrors and equally tried to fudge any vague promises of support for South Arabia. Balfour had promised to support the creation of a Jewish national 'heimat' in Palestine, a declaration that was scandalously ignored and which became an open sore in

Israeli-British relationships. Essentially, the English and French carved up Palestine and South Arabia. By the 1930s, Palestine resistance to both British control and Zionist settlements climaxed with an Arab revolt in 1939 with Zionist militia and complicit Arab states.

The British Government promised... we have learned to treat these offers with caution... to limit Jewish immigration and offer Palestine independence in ten years.

Meanwhile, Pauline and her crew were in the front line. "One day, the alarm went. A sergeant gave me a machine gun. I asked him, 'Have I got to fire this, Sarge?' He told me to balance it on the wall because I might need it – and suddenly I saw more Arabs in turbans than I had ever seen in my life. The desert isn't flat. It's full of shifting sand dunes of different sizes and shapes and the Arabs hide behind them. They were coming towards us. They had guns and they were starting to fire. I just stood there.

The squaddie next to me said, 'Fire. FIRE YOUR GUN.' Alright – I did. I shot this Arab. He didn't get up. And then another started towards me, and I shot him. I must have shot about five of them. The squaddies were firing and throwing grenades. Luckily for us, a helicopter arrived and started firing down at the Arabs. They disappeared back into the sand dunes. I was motionless, I couldn't move. The Arabs that I had shot were lying on the ground. I knew I'd killed them. There were bodies everywhere. I don't know what went through my mind. The soldier asked if I was alright? I wasn't sure. I told him that I'd just killed five people. He said that I had no choice and that I had done 'bloody well'.

"I didn't know about that, but I do know I was a bit shell shocked afterwards. The Sergeant Major was brilliant. I was given a week's leave."

Pauline was commended for her actions and promoted to Lance Corporal. "It took me a long time to come to terms with killing people. It isn't what I was comfortable doing, but it was me or them. I have spoken to psychiatrists and have learnt to accept what had to be done."

From Pauline's album: wary British sentry and sullen guarded Arabs.

England eventually promised independence to the Federation of South Arabia in 1964. In June 1967, matters had progressed to the readings of 'Relinquishment of Sovereignty over Aden, Perim and Kuria Muria islands' Bill in the House of Commons. (Perim island is a small volcanic outpost in the Bab al Mandeb straits opposite Aden and Kuria Muria lies off the coast of Oman.)

The date for expected independence, 9 January 1968, would depend upon security against external aggression and 'freedom for the ordinary individual to live in conditions of normal law and order'. [1] It was becoming clear to everyone, even those isolated in Westminster, that 'conditions of law and order' in Aden, June 1967, were very far from normal.

Philip Goodhart's pious hope that a swift evacuation and handover would bring everyone to their senses and make the disparate and hostile elements in Aden and South Arabia work together could no longer be considered a valid argument.

Pauline could have told him that. From her switchboard, she knew something of the discussions between the Brigadiers involved in the front line. She could not know until much later, the details of battles over Aden which were taking place in Parliament. The debates in both Houses were long and fierce. In essence, the questions were simple. Should the British abandon Aden to the terrorists? Would our continuing military base help the Colony towards a smooth independence or hinder the formation of a new Federation? Could we move towards Independence when there was no constitutional internal governance? How should we treat the 80,000 citizens of Aden who were British subjects? Had we properly involved the United Nations, and were we consulting with the neighbouring territories and indeed Aden itself? Jeremy Thorpe put the position very neatly: 'we are being asked to give the Government a blank cheque to give up sovereignty when they want and there is to be no further consultation with the people in a Crown Colony with whom we have a most particular relationship... It must be the first time in a long and honourable history of liquidating a colonial Empire in which we deliberately give independence to a territory which is a Crown Colony in order that we may force them (Aden) into a federal structure to which many of its inhabitants are violently opposed.'

Philip Goodhart MP, knew that Nasser was likely to remain a threat. He also raised the question of oil supplies, the smooth flow of which was the reason for the British continuing interest in the Middle East. Pauline overheard conversations with senior Army personnel and became intrigued. Who really knew what was going on? Why had the High Commissioner, Sir Richard Turnbull, who had worked so long and hard to make the South Arabia Federation a reality, been replaced and why was diplomat Sir Humphrey Trevelyan taking over?

Turnbull later felt betrayed by the British Labour Party, especially Foreign Secretary George Brown. Rumours swirled. Apparently, Trevelyan had formed 'amicable' links with Nasser during his last posting in Egypt, strengthening the eventual stories that England had 'bought off' the NLF to ease military evacuation on independence. There is no doubt that covert diplomacy and undercover operations were taking place alongside the formal Parliamentary business. An old story exists which explains that the sun never set on the British Empire because God didn't trust the English in the dark...

Nasser on a sofa, not having an easy time with the British. Not surprising. Anthony Eden on right. But were we supporting Egypt or Palestine or Israel?

Later, Pauline would undertake personal research into the Parliamentary debates during March, April and June 1967 and collect the Hansard accounts relating to Aden. She needed to understand the background to the conversations between senior military personnel and English government officials in Whitehall for herself.

Meanwhile, just driving down Murder Mile to work on the switchboard was a daily challenge. "One day, we saw about 150 Arabs piling rocks on the other side of the concrete wall. We knew when we drove up that section that we'd find an ambush and it looked bad. A new recruit in the lorry was holding his gun with safety catch off. I took it away from him, thinking he looked too nervous. I told him not to shoot us. One of the girls was crying, hysterically. I decided I would get out. The Arabs weren't sure about white women. They'd never seen one. They thought we might be something from Allah which made them wary. Would Allah be angry if they injured us? Adrenalin kicked in. I wanted to get to work. I told the screaming girl that she was useless and would she please shut up. I picked up my gun and marched out of the Land Rover towards the Arabs. I shouted all sorts of newly learnt obscenities about what Allah would and wouldn't do if they didn't move all those rocks and let us go. We had radioed for help and I have to tell you that I was never so pleased to see that ferret gun drive down the other side of the road. I'm still hurling insults at them, but when they saw the gun, they started clearing the road and moving the rocks away. I got back in the Land Rover and we drove to the telephone exchange to get to work. I told all the girls on the switchboard about the fun we'd had – and that there was every possibility they would meet it on the way back."

Strictly speaking, Lance Corporal Cole was a switchboard operator – but she was also female Army staff. Only women were appropriate for searching and checking the Arab women for bomb-making materials and bombs themselves, all too easily concealed under niquab and abayas.

The British Government never knew anything about it. Lord Segal, debating Aden in July 1967, asked if 'whether it was true that many instances occurred of Moslem women coming through the check points of Sheikh Othman being known to have large numbers of hand grenades in their flowing black robes and yet our troops have not been allowed to search them?' Pauline could have told the House that they were, and she did.

Here is Pauline, 2nd from right, with some colleagues on the Aden beach between switchboard duties: it looked fun but danger was never very faraway.

"On those days, we had to be ready for 6 a.m. when an armed escort would take us to a particular village. Squaddies removed the men and stood guarding them with a gun; all that was left were the women and children. We didn't have a gun. We searched a couple of tents and found nothing, and then in the third, there were three women, grandmother, mother and daughter. I can't tell you how filthy everything is. I know water is scarce and they are primitive, but they really stank. I searched them and went all through the bedding and the blankets. 'I don't think there's anything here, Sarge.'

He said, 'You've missed something, Corporal.' He was right

– I hadn't checked a little baby, about ten months old, with bandages around his eyes. He told me to unwrap the bandage. The mother tried to go for me but a colleague grabbed her. I couldn't believe what I saw. The little boy had a cockroach in each eye. They had been placed there to eat his eyes. I took them out, and flung them to the floor. The sergeant said, 'She'll do it again as soon as you're gone. She'll do it because when he's four, he will be blind and he will be able to beg for food.' What did I do? I hit her. I wanted to kill her.

"The sergeant told me there was nothing we could do that interfered with their religion or way of life. He promised he wouldn't say anything about me beating her up. I learned that Arab women can maim their babies by bending their soft limbs together. Once deformed, a child can attract attention and beg. I don't have a lot of time for the Arabs."

Fighting in Aden; not always easy to know who was the enemy.

Mostly, British troops moved around in armoured cars, Land Rovers with tin tops and always guarded by armed soldiers. Sometimes, they drove in a PIG, a heavily armoured vehicle resembling a small tank on tyres. It had mounted guns and window slits for the driver. But even a PIG was not proof against the possibility of a grenade exploding underneath it. A favourite ploy of the Arab terrorists was to hide among the shifting sand dunes and roll grenades towards any vehicle that approached. Mostly, nothing much happened, but, as Pauline recalls, "Once, they got us. The grenade hit us squarely underneath and the PIG rolled slowly down a bank. I was more concerned about the bloke in the observation turret with his head sticking out, but he got back in time. Nobody was injured although we were fairly battered and bruised: we weren't sitting on cushions! We couldn't get out of the door and our only exit would have been through the turret, but the officer said we were safer inside. Crawling out one by one would have made us very easy targets to be picked off by the snipers. We had radioed for reinforcements and a helicopter arrived as well as a three tonner and a pack of soldiers. We were given three days leave."

From The Guardian, February 20th, 1967.

Northumberland Fusiliers keep watch over Crater whilst men of the 45, Marine Commandos search for terrorists in a Radfan mountain village. The adjacent report on reducing the size of the army relates to West German reluctance to offset foreign exchange costs of the Rhine army.

CHAPTER THREE

Pauline, interviewed by the Imperial War Museum and indeed by this narrator, tells stories in a straightforward and disciplined fashion. The Imperial War Museum have recorded several hours of tape recorded history from Pauline whose experiences from the front line in Aden are now considered part of military history. But Pauline might have been describing a Sunday picnic. At no point in the extremely hazardous months in Aden does she ever fail in her duty or ever allow fear or fright to dominate the situation. Her worst nightmares happened when friends and colleagues suffered danger – or worse.

The School Run: children became used to armed escorts in 1960s Aden.

"One day we'd done a village search and were returning to base with two Land Rovers, two 3 tonners and a ferret gun. The road was hot and apparently endless. Suddenly, I blinked.

There was a very loud bang. The Land Rover driving in front had gone. Disappeared. There were metal scraps all over the road and bits of body but you didn't sit in the Land Rover and scream. You went into action automatically. That was training. I jumped out and ran forward. Six squaddies in the back seemed to be safe. But the driver and a passenger in the front seat were blown to bits. I found a pulse on one soldier and shouted for a medic. I looked down and saw that he had a leg missing. The doctor came and took over. I understand that he survived. We collected every single body part we could, as reverently as possible. I never wanted to leave any part of a British soldier behind. I'll never forget picking up bits of arm, leg, flesh, fingers: I couldn't bear to think we'd forgotten any part of anyone." Bodies, whole or otherwise, had to be buried as fast as possible in the dust and heat of the Middle East. Freezers were an undreamt of luxury and the base was too far from England to allow coffins to return home for burial. Plaques were erected over burial sites in the sand and the sacred spots were protected as far as possible – but Pauline mourns the lack of proper care for soldiers killed in battle. Something she feels especially strongly is the destruction of all the cemeteries in the sand when the British finally pulled out of the base.

"We had to blow them up. I was very, very sad about it. I telephoned the Brigadier in Guildford and requested permission to find out why. She told me that the Arabs would have gone in and desecrated the graves. We couldn't have left anything behind. I felt dreadful for the parents of those soldiers. We lost nearly three hundred soldiers and there is nowhere tangible as a focus of grief for their families.

"We cleaned up the road and drove back to base. I was told to stand at ease, and instructed to take a shower and rest for a while. My hatred of the Arabs was so intense that I wanted to kill all of them. Did I want to talk about it? Post traumatic stress disorder was unheard of in those days, but we understood that sharing experiences often helped. I was offered help, but I didn't think I needed it. You just carried on. I kept most of it to myself.

"Back at work on the switchboard, we always knew when a major incident happened – it lit up like the Blackpool illuminations. We would start answering 'flash' calls which were the equivalent of 999. Well, on 20 June 1967, everything was going up in lights. Brigadiers were telephoning Brigadiers to say that the Arabs had gone into Crater. Apparently, the Arab police had switched sides and joined the militants. The insurgents suddenly attacked and in the fierce fighting, twenty-eight soldiers had been killed, thirty-nine soldiers were injured and the hospital needed blood. Everyone not on duty was rushed to the hospital. The Arabs shot soldiers in the legs so that they couldn't run away. They disembowelled them alive. Then they threw the bodies, half alive or half dead, into the Land Rovers and set them alight. We sat on the hospital beds of the survivors and held their hands as they cried. Some of the stories were horrendous. We learnt that Colonel Mitchell was watching the attack from air and saw all the black smoke, but he didn't realise that British soldiers were being burned alive."

Aden, Helicopters in action.

Pauline found herself unwittingly at the centre of one of the most controversial military actions in modern history. She had Colonel Mitchell on the telephone and retained sufficient presence of mind to commiserate. 'I'm very sorry to hear about all the men you've lost, Sir,' she said.

'Thank you very much, my dear,' was the reply.

"Colonel Mitchell asked to be put through to the Prime Minister, Harold Wilson. My job was to listen in and take notes, if necessary. Basically, the Colonel told Wilson that the Arabs had taken over Crater and they've killed twenty-eight soldiers and injured dozens more. Colonel Mitchell said he wanted to go in and recapture Crater. The Prime Minister said he was not to do anything of the sort. 'That is an order. You are to take a step back, Colonel Mitchell. You are not to recapture Crater.' Colonel Mitchell hung up on him. I was left with the Prime Minister on the telephone. I had to apologise. 'I'm ever so sorry, Sir, I seem to have lost the line to Colonel Mitchell. I'm ever so sorry.' I knew he had hung up, but I couldn't say so."

The story was headlines in the British Press. '17 British Soldiers killed in Aden' was front page in The Guardian, for 21 June. 'Mutineers free prisoners' was underneath, in huge type. Apparently, the South Arabian troops had mutinied in protest against the disciplinary suspension of four Arab Colonels. Warders were forced at gunpoint to open the doors of the town's prison and 169 prisoners believed to have escaped.

The Arabs were jubilant. Seizing Crater was a major victory against the occupying forces and a huge boost to terrorist morale. British soldiers were forced to withdraw completely from the town, and remained on observation posts on the hills around. Barriers had been placed at the two entrances to Crater but otherwise, no retaliatory action was immediately forthcoming. Colonel Mitchell explains in his book that 'the view of British higher command was that any attempt to retake Crater would have to be made in very considerable force, using heavy weapon support. They feared that this would cause heavy casualties to the armed police and possibly to civilians'. They continued this gloomy appreciation by suggesting that in such an event, the South Arabia army and the police would mutiny 'to a man', a statement that Colonel Mitchell understood to be the ultimate Committee prevarication.

General Officer Commanding Middle East Land Forces was one Major-General Philip Tower. He believed that regaining Crater would cause more problems than it solved. He also considered that a full reoccupation of Crater was pointless given that the British withdrawal from Aden was imminent. Major-General Tower did authorise an investigation into Crater led by Mitchell with the Argylls, a small gesture of permission which Colonel Mitchell expanded into a full scale operation.

Mitchell went into attack – political style. He telephoned everyone possible to enlist support for the recapture of Crater. Some backed him, some refused. As far as he was concerned, the pride of the British Empire was at stake. Mitchell wanted the British to display a 'bit of grit'. He became irritated with a Government that put politics before soldiering and a Government that had no knowledge of the Arabs and barely a thought for the Empire. He was certain that the longer the authorities dillydallied, the longer it would give rebel forces time to build up their defences. He had allies and he hatched a plan. Called Operation Stirling Castle, it was to be a bold entry into Crater, accompanied by his regiment of Argyll and Southern Highlanders in full swirling kit, and playing bagpipes.

With terrific courage and incredible *sang froid*, Colonel Mitchell dodged machine guns, strode into the centre of the town and explained to the Arabs that they were going to reoccupy the buildings. Their aim was peaceful but determined. There would be no bloodshed. This was not an eye for an eye, although all were conscious of recent death. It worked. Only one life was lost, and that by an Arab sniper. Most of the Arabs ran away. The Aden police apologised for switching sides and explained that they had been threatened by the militants and they didn't have a choice. But Mitchell wasn't taking any chances and they were locked up in a prison camp.

In action: Colonel Mitchell at the wheel during the advance into Crater, July 1967.

Once Crater had been restored to British rule, Colonel Mitchell employed some controversially strong arm tactics to keep order. The manner in which he achieved control was described as 'extremely firm and extremely mean'. 'Argylls Law' as it was dubbed, operated by house to house searches, summary executions and enforced curfews. This was criticised as maintaining order and discipline at the expense of generating trust and allegiance of the indigenous population long term.

Back at the switchboard, Pauline heard it all. She knew that the Labour Government were trying to squeeze out Defence Minister Denis Healey who would have supported Colonel Mitchell. She became aware of the conflict between the soldiery and the Government. Matters seemed to have passed from the House of Commons to the House of Lords when Lord Shackleton, Minister without Portfolio, was appointed as special envoy in Aden. His fact finding missions accomplished a great deal more than the interparty bickering which characterised political debates in Aden earlier in the year. Unlike both the Labour Party and indeed the United Nations, Shackleton understood that any British military presence in South Arabia would be to deter external aggression against South Arabia and not to perpetuate historical dominance by the former Empire.

Terrorist bombs in Aden.
From the Aden Veterans Photo Gallery.

Colonel Mitchell may have been a controversial character for his political bosses or military superiors, but he became a darling of the British press. Suddenly, England had a military hero and the newspapers went wild. He was dubbed 'Mad Mitch', an inappropriate nickname for a brave man of principle and it did him no favours in the years to come. He appeared to be fighting not just Arab insurgents but toadying politicians on the make. Tales of derring-do in far-flung outposts of the Empire made an irresistible story and BBC and ITV news channels carried constant reports of the dashing soldier and his gloriously attired Argyll and Sutherland Highlanders. Questions were asked in Parliament. Tam Dalyell (Labour, West Lothian) asked if it was true that Mitchell had disobeyed the operational and administrative orders of his senior officers during the recapture of Crater? It seemed that politicians had forgotten Nelson putting the telescope to his blind eye.

In the House of Lords, Earl Jellicoe took Mitchell's side. On 17 July 1967, Jellicoe stood up to say 'I should like, first of all, to join with the noble Lord, Lord Shackleton, in expressing our admiration for the skill and efficiency which has enabled our re-occupation of Crater to be carried out with the minimum of casualties. It was a very remarkable and skilfully executed operation.'

The Guardian told it straight. On 3 July a UPI report described how; 'British troops tonight reoccupied Crater Town which was seized more than two weeks ago by rebellious Arab nationalists. The troops, taking cover behind armoured vehicles, moved into the mile-square maze of alleys and took up the strong points they had held before the revolt. There was little resistance. Only one Arab was known to have been killed. 'We had been expecting much stiffer resistance' said a British officer.

Arab nationalists had held Crater since fighting broke out between British troops and mutinous Arab police. British forces had contented themselves with watching traffic moving in and out. 'Militarily, the situation is intolerable,' a British officer said shortly before the troops moved in.'

The fall of Crater to the Arabs was a setback for British plans for a smooth transition to independence the next year for it produced a sharp conflict between the Colony's British military and civilian administrators. The Army wanted to retake Crater by force. The civilians preferred to wait and see if the resistance collapsed. Until today, the civilians had their way.

The Guardian, July 5th, 1967. The national newspaper report from Reuters explained that 'British troops were now in a reasonable position to take care of anything. Major

General Philip Tower said that the armed Arab police who led the nationalist revolt two weeks ago were not 'frightfully pleased' about the takeover, but were cooperating with British troops. General Tower said the troops had returned to Crater to ensure that life could remain as normal as possible'.

"All the talk in the NAAFI or the Exclusive Club focused on the recapture of Crater. The soldiers had nothing but admiration for Colonel Mitchell. We thought he was utterly amazing. I began to feel contempt for the British Government under Harold Wilson who I believe was a very weak man. The Labour Government were friendly with Saudi Arabia because Saudi Arabia had oil. They didn't want anything to do with Aden, it had become a nuisance that they wanted to be rid of. Aden didn't have anything they thought we wanted. But you can't lose 150 years of tradition just like that and the strategic point of Aden was always there."

Federation of South Arabia flag.

Losing 150 years of tradition in Aden was exactly what the Labour Government did want to do. It was hamstrung by Conservative opposition who did not accept that Aden's internal constitution was ready to maintain security and stability by the proposed date for independence, 8 January 1968. Terrorism had frozen the constitution of democratic rule in Aden since September 1966. For almost two years, there had been almost complete stagnation in political and constitutional spheres. Commissions and conferences called for by Colonial Secretaries and United Nations Representatives to advance constitutional security in Aden somehow never happened. Questions in Parliament relating to the South Arabian Army's ability to repulse a full scale Egyptian attack, were ducked by Harold Wilson. The Conservative MP Peter Tapsell spoke for many when he declared that 'we should tell the world that Aden is a British responsibility which we intend to discharge without foreign interference and that we had a moral duty to maintain our forces in the area until we can guarantee a stable government'.

Alec Douglas Home managed to defer the decisions on a date to leave Aden by insisting that more time be given for a full statement of policy.

The debates on Aden during the summer of 1967 degenerated into a political tennis match. Both sides appeared to use Aden as a sports field. They fought for advantages relating to leadership of their particular parties in schoolboy language.

Foreign Secretary George Brown's vocabulary was rude and basic. He accused Duncan Sandys of having the skin of a rhinoceros. Brown couldn't imagine anyone wanting to lead the Tories whilst the Labour William Molloy accused them of disliking the United Nations and prejudicing neutral third party intervention.

Jeremy Thorpe, with no interest in leading either the Conservatives or the Labour Party, felt that it was a question of time. He believed that Aden itself was being pushed into a Federal structure to which many people in the Colony were opposed, as well as many in Parliament. 'There are many people in Aden with views as to what they want to do on independence and they do not all want to join the South Arabian Federation. Will they be given any opportunity to express that view or will they be dragooned into the Federation in the same way as this Government hope to dragoon us?' Thorpe believed that neither the House nor the

Colony of Aden had been sufficiently consulted or briefed, and there appeared no plans to do either.

Shopping in the markets, Aden style.

CHAPTER FOUR

In one of the constant news reports from Aden in 1967, Cliff Michelmore and the BBC Twenty Four Hours crew filmed some of the military training at the base. Pauline was selected to demonstrate life-saving swimming: the plan was for a girl to 'fall in' to a swimming pool and be 'rescued' by Pauline. It isn't as easy as it sounds. Drowning people push themselves up on their rescuers with terrific force and the process can be as dangerous for the rescuer as for the swimmer in trouble. All went well until the producer decided to play a trick. He made one of his camera crew jump into the pool. Then he shouted at Pauline. 'Someone's drowning,' yelled the producer. 'He really can't swim! Help, help'.

Pauline rushed to the rescue. "I just dived in. I never thought twice. I didn't even know they were filming. I tore over to this chap and he was really fighting me. I grabbed his hair and got him on his back, and then tugged him to safety at the side of the pool. And then he swam back to the other side, if you please! I was flabbergasted. I said, that's not fair! Michelmore and his crew were delighted and thanked me for a fantastic film, so I couldn't be too cross. He wanted my home telephone number in England so that he could let my parents know when the programme would be transmitted. My family told everyone they knew and all the neighbours and all the aunts and uncles watched my face on television – apparently, it was quite a close-up and in some detail!"

But if Pauline was winning a new audience of admirers, Colonel Mitchell was a worrying threat for the British Government. It wasn't just that he appeared to have exceeded his authority, although that was bad enough: there began to be allegations concerning the behaviour of the Argyll and Sutherland Highlanders. The soldiers had used the Chartered Bank building in Crater as their headquarters and snipers on the roof picked off any Arab seen as dangerous in the street below.

Apparently, Colonel Mitchell described it as shooting grouse – a brace here, a brace there. Mitchell's critics complained that he was a publicity seeker and that the troops under his command lacked discipline. One High Commission described the Argylls as a 'bunch of Glasgow thugs' (a statement for which he later apologised). But the Daily Telegraph took a very different view: 'the British troops have shown the combination of skill, tact and cool courage for which they are unequalled by regaining the Crater district of Aden, thus a dangerous and humiliating state of drift, which the British Government permitted to continue for a fortnight, has been ended. The longer this lasted, the more credible did the terrorist boast become that Britain would be driven out of Aden before independence.'

Although Colonel Mitchell was responsible for bringing the Arabs to heel in Crater with a subsequent barrage of publicity, many terrorist murders had gone largely unreported in the Western press. Pauline was aware that the British Government did not want news of Arab atrocities and some of the more appalling incidents were swept under the carpet. She recalls one particularly horrible incident which demonstrated the vicious cruelty of guerrilla warfare.

"Little Aden was connected to Aden proper, or Big Aden, by a narrow causeway about two miles long. It was closed at dusk and guarded by ferret guns at either end so that no Arabs could lay bombs on the isthmus: divers went down either side morning and evening to check that no lymph mines had been laid alongside the foundations. The SAS had several operatives in Aden, superbly camouflaged as Arabs in every respect. They were tanned, fluent in Arabic and able to infiltrate the terrorist/communist networks and obtain vital intelligence. On the switchboard, we learned that two SAS men were missing. For a little while, there was no news of them at all. And then, one morning, when the ferret gun opened up the causeway to Little Aden, the driver saw something lying on the way ahead. Nervously, he investigated. It was part of a soldier. The Arabs had killed the two SAS officers, carved them into pieces and spread the body parts over the two miles of causeway. No one knows how they did it without being seen.

Narrow connecting causeway between Little Aden and Aden.

"Colonel Mitchell was on the telephone at once. He demanded an investigation. He couldn't persuade anyone to bother. Most of the Brigadiers were sitting on their verandahs drinking whisky in the sunshine, thinking they were going home soon. The British Government simply didn't want to know."

Pauline met Colonel Mitchell and was in his thrall forever. Like every soldier, she admired his fearless demeanour and his moral courage. If he believed that a course of action was the right one, he upheld it, no matter the consequences. "He may have been small in stature," says Pauline, "but he was huge in presence and charisma." Defenders of Mitchell are inevitably critical of Harold Wilson and the Labour Government. Pauline believes that Wilson was a very weak and effective man. "When Colonel Mitchell told him what was going on, he didn't want to know. He hushed up the killing of British soldiers in Aden. He was Prime Minister, he should have called a Cabinet meeting, or involved senior politicians. He just ordered Colonel Mitchell not to go in and recapture Crater."

His men thought the world of him: Mitchell with the Argylls.

But if Pauline feels angry at the Government's attitude to an historic British base held by British troops, she was outraged by the treatment of Colonel Mitchell personally. The gallant soldier was 'allowed' to leave the Army immediately instead of serving out the remainder of his term once resignation had been offered in 1967 and demoted from Lt. Colonel to plain Mr Colin Mitchell. "Even the Brigadiers said it was wrong not to allow him to remain Colonel Mitchell. As a civilian, Colin Mitchell continued to fight to keep his regiment of Argyll and Sutherland Highlanders going, but they were disbanded in 1968." It is curious that Colin Mitchell's name does not appear in many subsequent accounts of the Aden Emergency.

CHAPTER FIVE

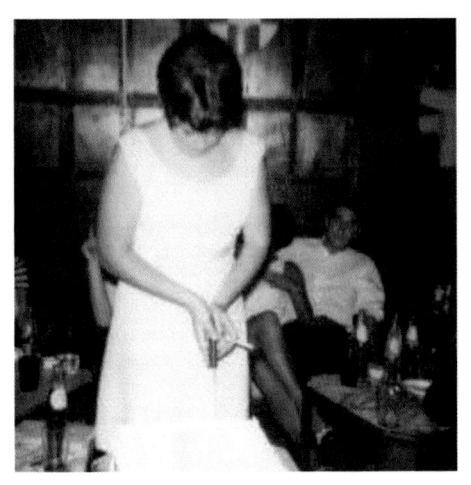

Cutting her cake – Pauline's coming of age in Aden.

On 25 July 1967, Pauline celebrated her twenty-first birthday. Her parents sent a congratulatory telegram which she still keeps, carefully mounted in an album, along with photographs of dances and parties in the mess. There were just forty army women serving on the base, twenty on switchboard duties and the remaining twenty working in medical, secretarial or administrative roles. Pauline describes how army women generally didn't get involved in active service fighting terrorists: "No one wanted headlines like Army Girl Killed in Aden, although of course daily life could be hazardous enough without looking for trouble. I found myself on the front line with a gun – I remember some bumptious Colonel on Sky News claiming that no armed women were ever on active service and I wanted to ring him up and shout at him. I was! Now of course women are trained alongside men which I think is amazing. I would have loved that. Some of us had other ideas. Once, two girls went AWOL (absent without leave) in the desert and the army found them in a Sheikh's harem. They didn't want to come back. They wanted to stay with the Sheikh. We couldn't just go in and get them out. The tents were like embassies, as well as being magnificent structures. We left them there, and, as far as I know, perfectly happily. I often wonder what happened to them. It was a risky business, miles away in the middle of nowhere...

"If we were off duty, we had to wear long skirts and covered tops. We always walked about in pairs. Arabs stared at us, but they were quite happy to see us in the bazar, we might spend money. The jewellery and the silks were beautiful. I didn't know enough Arabic to ask for a dress to be made. So I drew a picture. The Arab never touched me, just indicated that I should turn around slowly. He told me to return in three days. The dress fitted me perfectly. Another occasion was less straightforward.

"The shops were like garages, with pull-down shutters to lock up. Two of us were just wandering through the bazaar. We entered into one shop and we were just looking around when three Arabs pulled the shutters down behind us. I thought, ooh, now what. I grabbed my colleague and we stood with our backs to the wall. The Arabs started walking towards us, and they didn't look too friendly. The other girl started screaming. I told her to throw anything she could pick up at them – baked beans, cuddly toys, anything on the shelves. I was hurling stuff at them, when all of a sudden, I saw two pairs of Army boots, just visible in the gap between the shutters and the sand. Up came the shutters and in came the paras! I was never so pleased to see a couple of soldiers in my life. I didn't actually know what the Arabs were going to do. If the Arabs had been white, they would have gone whiter still. They started gibbering in Arabic. The paras yanked us out, went in and pulled the shutters down behind them. We could hear the most almighty banging and clattering. When they eventually came out, dusting themselves down, I asked what they'd done. What did you expect us to do, they said, smiling. They drove us home. It was a chastening experience.

"Actually, I don't think they meant to hurt us. They were just fascinated by white women. They had never seen them. All Arab women are dark, I'm light brown and my colleague had fair, curly hair. I suppose it's just as well that my colleague started screaming, or the paras would never have known we were there." The impression remains that Pauline could have coped with the Arabs single handed, without the aid of the paras, if she hadn't had a screaming girl alongside. She was always more than a match for most.

On 19 November 1967, the British Government decided on an ultimate withdrawal of British forces in Aden. George Brown, head of the Foreign Office wrote that : 'there is no evidence that we could achieve anything useful to the Arabs or ourselves... the problems are no longer ones in which outside powers should remain to play a part. We should, as soon as possible, leave the Arabs to sort their own problems without the complications of military personnel.'

He might have added that although the Government looked like saving £30 million pounds a year they would be allowing the National Liberation Front victory in South Yemen, with the possibility of establishing a lone Marxist state in the Middle East. Any remnants of the original Federation of South Arabia, fled abroad or were assassinated in the last few tumultuous months of British occupation.

Pauline never forgot her flight home. She was on the last British aeroplane to leave the base. Once again, there appeared to be no stewardesses, only stewards on the aeroplane. As she took her seat, a glass was put into her hand. 'This is from seat 53,' she was told. 'And this is from seat 74.

Please have a drink, and thank you! Here is a token from seat 65.' "It went on for an hour and I couldn't drink them all. When we landed at Heathrow, six o'clock in the morning, two men from airport security came on board. Apparently the press had learned that an Army girl from Aden was on the aeroplane and they were very keen to speak to me. I knew that no one of my rank was ever allowed to talk to the press without an officer present – and I also knew that I was a little tiddly. You would be, after all those kind tokens from total strangers on the flight. I felt very important! I was whisked to a VIP lounge for coffee and something to eat before being smuggled away in a limousine with blacked-out windows. I never was allowed to meet the reporters, but I know what I would have said. I was very angry with the Labour Party's handling of the situation. How could they write off a hundred years of British history just like that? They wanted to keep Saudi Arabia happy because Saudi Arabia had oil. Aden didn't have anything they wanted any more. It was a carbuncle for Harold Wilson and he wanted to chop it off.

"It was 28 November, the date of my mother's birthday. I was taken to Euston station to catch a train to Apsley. Hemel Hempstead seemed to have happened in my absence. But Apsley was my destination. I knew the stationmaster and everybody else, most of them played bowls with my Dad. The taxi driver who collected me from the station said, 'Hello Pauline, back on leave?'

"It was the middle of the day and both my parents were at work. I wanted to surprise them. I knew Mum usually left a small window open. After some difficulty, I managed to jump up and the taxi driver shoved me through. I telephoned Dickinsons' and spoke to Miss Laing, the supervisor. 'Could you put me through to Mrs Cole, please?'

"Mum came on the line. I wished her a very happy birthday. 'Are you calling from Aden, dear?' she said. I told her I was in her sitting room, using her telephone. There was a strange, rumbling noise, and Miss Laing told me that she'd fainted away. She got hold of Dad and Dickinsons' sent them home at once in a car. They walked through the door and – well – you can guess. It was just lovely."

Everyone wanted some of Pauline's time when she got home. She hadn't been back for a year and there were a great many aunts, uncles, friends and family members who wanted to see her and enjoy feeling proud of the brave and courageous young girl in their midst. Still only twenty-one, she seemed to have had more lives than any of them already: her desire for adventure had been more than fulfilled – so far. It left its mark: Pauline never forgot standing outside Woolworths in the new Hemel Hempstead with her mother when a car back-fired. Instinctively, she hurled her mother to the pavement and flung herself on top of her. "Mother was very embarrassed. She was going, 'Pauline what ARE you doing? In front of all these people?' I got her up, but all her tights were ripped and her clothes were torn. Father was in hysterics."

Pauline's Mum.

"I was itching to get back. The village where I grew up seemed to have become very small. I was given six weeks leave before my next posting to Bielefeld, in North Germany."

Bielefeld was a very different kettle of fish to Aden. It had become the headquarters for the British Army on the Rhine, (BAOR) after the end of the Second World War, and its role was administrative and strategic rather than aggressive or territorial. No German was ever likely to become insurgent after 1945: one of the strangest facts of this period of history was how the Nazis disappeared from the face of the earth after the death of Adolf Hitler.

Bielefeld: slap bang in the middle of Germany.

But the Yalta Conference which organised the division of Germany post 1945 decreed that an occupying force should remain in North Rhine-Westphalia and Bielefeld, on the main east-west autobahn, was the logical place. It had long been an army town and sizeable barracks remained from their original construction in the 1930s.

Pauline, now promoted to Corporal Cole, returned to Guildford to be fitted out with new uniforms. She had lost weight in Aden – more serious was the development of melanoma, traced to her duties in the hot Middle Eastern climate. In the early 1960s, sunshine was believed to be beneficial and sunblock creams had not been either developed or thought necessary. "I wore a bikini whenever I could – we were on the beach at every opportunity. No one understood the dangers of radiation – nor that it can remain undetected in the body for years. Eventually, I went for consultation to the MOD and received a large cheque for compensation." Less tangible than radiation and equally unfamiliar in the 1960s were the psychiatric horrors of post traumatic stress disorder. Pauline suffered considerably from the shock of losing friends and colleagues. "I still think about Aden a lot. I'll never forget watching the switchboard light up in emergency and just praying that someone I knew wasn't killed or seriously injured. I couldn't go down to the cemetery, I didn't always have time and we always needed an escort. Sometimes, I didn't know their names, but I knew their laughter in the NAAFI."

Bielefeld should have been a peaceful posting – but there were problems as Pauline very soon discovered. "It's difficult to occupy part of a country in peacetime. We were obliged to employ a certain number of local people and although they needed the work, they tended to resent us. The entire sixteen-position switchboard was operated by German women under the supervision of Frau Zarber.

"They mainly spoke German which produced complaints from barracks all over Germany. So the Royal Corps of Signals were sent in to run the switchboard and I was the first up. I was warned that I wouldn't have an easy time of it. Frau Zarber saw me as a threat –I was a threat.

Bielefeld, North Western Germany.

"On the first day, I walked into the switchboard office. I was wearing my uniform. Frau Zarber sat behind the desk and all the operators turned round to check the new recruit. If looks could kill, I'd have been dead in seconds. Frau Zarber ignored me. I saw an empty post and sat down. Nobody talked to me, no one even said hello. I watched what the girl at the adjacent post was doing, but I couldn't speak enough German to ask for help. After about three days of this, Major Maine called me in. He was a brilliant officer and we had an excellent rapport. 'Corporal Cole,' he asked. 'How are you getting on.'

"I confessed that I was struggling. 'No one talks to me, no one lets me plug in, I can't learn either the switchboard or the language.'

"Major Maine was reassuring. 'Leave it to me,' he said. The following day, Frau Zarber actually spoke to me, and instructed me to 'sit there'. I plugged in and off I went. After about three months, I was able to speak basic German and to understand a great deal more. But my English voice was always a relief. I'd say, 'Bielefeld 35,' to a Colonel or a Brigadier from another camp and their voices would shine with relief. 'Are you English?' they would ask. 'Thank God for that!'

"Three months later, an English contingent arrived and I trained them at the switchboard. After six or seven months, Major Maine called me in again. 'You're improperly dressed, Sergeant Cole.' Sergeant! Promotion! He handed me my stripes.

"Now that was something I could never do. 'Sir,' I protested, 'I can't sew!' One of the other girls sewed them on for me. When I returned to the switchboard, everyone cheered. Frau Zarber had disappeared: in the time that it had taken for me to receive my promotion and sew stripes on to my jacket, she had given in her notice and left. I was running the Bielefeld switchboard. I was on my own: I was in charge."

Sergeant's stripes, worn on the shoulder; officers have stars on their epaulettes.

1968 was not a comfortable time to be stationed anywhere near the Russian borders. As the Cold War escalated dangerously, Pauline's switchboard had a direct line to Berlin but in fact, Czechoslovakia was of more immediate communist concern than Germany. Anton Dubcek's liberal government ended censorship early in 1968 and this new freedom inspired broad based support for reform. Suddenly, it was possible for government and party politics to be openly debated in a public sphere although there was never a question of abandoning completely the Marxist/Lenin economic system – communism. Nevertheless, Soviet leaders were alarmed by Dubcek, recalling the chaos of the Hungarian uprising in 1956: they feared that satellite states in the Eastern Europe might follow suit and inspire widespread rebellion against Moscow's leadership of the Eastern bloc.

The Warsaw Pact invasion in August 1968, caught Czechoslovakia and most of the Western world by surprise. Military 'exercises' had moved quantities of troops from the Soviet Union as well as certain numbers from Hungary, Poland, Bulgaria and East Germany who were then primed to take control of Prague, other major cities and communication and transport links. It was swift, ruthless and effective. It also laid down a doctrine which troubled the West ever since – that Moscow had the right to intervene with force in any country where a communist government was threatened.

Bielefield went on standby. The switchboard lit up like Blackpool. Pauline put her arm up in the air, recognised signal for a 'flash call', telephone equivalent of an urgent 999. "We were sent to the Quartermasters for green/beige warfare clothing, tin helmets and backpacks. Three 3 ton lorries were ready to evacuate the base, should it prove necessary. Major Maine called us in for a briefing. We had already signed the Official Secrets Act. He told us it was getting a bit serious – we knew this was English for 'become deadly'. All the barrack buildings were wired to be blown up in the event of invasion. My switchboard, I remember asking? The answer was yes. Everything was to be reduced to rubble. There must be nothing left. We would be whisked away in an army lorry.

"I was always intrigued by the Parade Ground. It was much, much larger than it needed to be. At this point, my curiosity got the better of me. I asked Major Maine. 'Sir. What's underneath the Parade Ground?'

"The Major looked at me carefully. 'You're a bit sharp, Sergeant Cole. There are rockets under that square. It opens up.' I knew it: not that it did me any good, and I don't know if it's still there. I don't think they ever fired the rockets. Rumours flew thick and fast, even though the rockets didn't. The Russians squashed Czechoslovakia and then the Chinese decided to go for Russia. We were left alone, armed and ready, but thankfully, we never had to put it to the test. We were told that if Russia ever did decide to mount a nuclear attack on Germany, we'd be the first to go, and we'd never know anything about it. Blink – and we'd be gone."

Once the Russians were diverted from Germany by China, life in Bielefeld returned to normal peacetime occupation. Pauline enjoyed her posting, so much so that she asked her parents if she could remain in Germany instead of going home on leave. (They didn't mind.) Together with twenty or so friends, she hired a three ton lorry, borrowed tents and went camping in the Black Forest. Wearing civilian clothes, she tramped miles through the spectacular countryside and the party went almost as far as Switzerland.

"We got along fine with the German people as long as they thought we were tourists. Once they knew we were military, it was another matter. I think they resented us being there – they demonstrated it by only speaking German."

Pauline was offered the opportunity to visit Auschwitz. She never forgot the experience. "Even now, just thinking about it makes the hairs on my arms stand up. Apparently, birds fly round the camp, even now. They don't fly over it. I just imagine the millions and millions who died there, and I still feel the terror and horror of it all. We were still writing exams and I learnt the background to the concentration camps and the organised brutality, as well as the eugenic theories of Aryan breeding. I wanted to tear down all the buildings and grow flowers. The site was still raw in the 1960s, but we were instructed to take nothing away and leave nothing there.

"We were travelling as Army personnel and we visited Poland and Russia but we were very limited in what we were allowed to see. We were confined to our bus which meant we couldn't talk to anyone and we weren't encouraged to get out and about. Of course we heard stories about the KGB and we knew that some people simply disappeared. Their way of life seemed very hard, there was nothing in the shops and long queues for even the simplest daily foodstuffs."

Back at base camp, Pauline was soon making her mark outside the switchboard. Major Maine invited her for some weapons training. She had already learnt how to use a pistol, machine and automatic rifle in Aden and heavy arms were no novelty. Now, she would try her hand on the Bielefeld range with the Major. 'I've had some good reports on your firing,' he told her. 'Let's have a go.' It wasn't like shooting Arabs behind the sand dunes, but the exercise was daunting. Candidates must hold a pistol, walk down a narrow alleyway, and assess immediately if the cardboard figure that pops out before them is friend or foe and, if the latter, shoot them.

Ranges varied from fifty feet to a hundred and fifty feet. Needless to say, Pauline's reactions – and actions – were perfectly in order. "I was good at it," she admits. Rifle shooting competitions required the candidates to lay down on their stomachs and hold the weapon close to their heads to aim for a target. Pauline entered as one of just three girls in a field of soldiers from all over Germany. She won her section.

Pauline had always been a sporty girl and the Army gave her plenty of opportunity to shine. She swam for the Army, an ability which prompted her to apply for a three day white-water canoe trip. She had never been in a canoe in her life before and never expected to find poles dangling above the rapids through which the boats must steer a tight and hazardous passage. "It was much harder than I expected. I was told to keep upright with the paddles and use them to turn the boat up again if – or rather when – I capsized. The current against me was very fierce."

She had a better time with the serious 'war exercises'. Pauline was one of fifteen girls picked to join the men: dressed in combat gear and carrying backpacks, she crawled under barbed wire, rolled through obstacles in mud and generally had a cracking time. There was no quarter given to the girls. Everyone lived in equal discomfort with cold showers, tinned meals and bad jokes.

"The lads might play games with us and let our tents down, but it was all in such good spirits that we couldn't mind. If we got 'shot', we had to carry a yellow sticker saying 'dead' on it."

CHAPTER SIX

Although Pauline's abilities earned her roles outside the switchboard, her duties remained primarily army communication. She took this extremely seriously and, on one occasion, with hilarious consequences.

"Royalty often came to visit. Members of the Royal Family frequently acted as Honorary Colonels of particular battalions stationed in Germany and they would make trips to Bielefeld, or Munster, often quite informally.

"We had a direct line to England and if, for example, the Duke of Edinburgh, was coming to Germany, he might make a telephone call to Buckingham Palace. Well, one morning, I received a call from someone who claimed to be the Duke of Edinburgh. I hadn't been told he was in the country. I was quite polite. I said, 'Good morning, Sir, I believe you're the Duke of Edinburgh?' probably sounding as if I didn't believe a word of it.

He said, 'I think I am!'

Just then, the switchboard office door flew open and Major Maine came rushing in. 'I've just been told that the Duke of Edinburgh's in Germany.'

'I know,' I said. 'I've got him on the telephone.'

"I told the Duke I would connect him at once. 'I'll put you through straightaway, Sir. I do apologise for keeping you waiting. I've just been told you're here.' He was fine about the whole thing, no doubt he had a few laughs later. But it could have been a hoax. Sometimes, I found myself speaking to

Princess Ann who was always extremely nice and indeed to Prince Charles who tended to be more austere.

The Queen with Prince Philip, about the time he breezed into Bielefeld.

"We could have fun on the switchboard ourselves. It was the days of pirate radio ships and Radio Caroline was broadcasting pop music and quiz shows from offshore. The sixteen position board had six staff on duty in the evenings and in spare moments, we telephoned the station. Often, we won the quiz. 'It's Bielefeld, in Germany, AGAIN,' shouted Radio Caroline. Heavens knows what anyone out there thought we were doing."

Pauline's promotion to Sergeant put her in no little difficulty. Normally, a newly created Sergeant would be moved elsewhere as remaining in her position with new status could make life awkward for her colleagues. But it wasn't possible to replace her easily. (Perhaps it never was.)

None of the Corporals was strong enough to take her place. When she first walked into the Mess with her new stripes, thirty-five soldiers cheered. "They all knew me! The Sergeant-Major started shouting, 'That'll do! Have some respect for an officer!'

I said, 'That's alright, Sergeant-Major. They never gave me

any problems'."

Orderly Officers were regularly appointed from within the ranks to take charge for limited periods. Instantly recognisable by their red sashes, Orderly Officers made certain that drunk and disorderly soldiers were properly fed, that incidents were monitored, if necessary, by the military police and that the NAAFI was under supervision. Pauline was regularly appointed Orderly Officer. "The first day started quite well. I enjoyed bumping into some of my boyfriends who had to salute me because I was wearing a red sash! I had to salute back! Both of us giggled. 'Good Morning, Corporal', I declared, very grandly.

'Good Morning, Ma'am,' came the reply.

"The Sergeant-Major belonged to the old school which probably thought women ought to be pregnant, barefoot and in the kitchen. He always carried his baton tucked under the arm and he was a pain in the bum.

Pauline, left, at the wedding of Army colleagues.

"One day when I was Orderly Officer, I received a call from the Royal Military Police. There had been an incident in one of the clubs downtown. Now, Germany and Holland in those days, were far more – how shall I put this – sexually liberated than we were. Prostitution was legal. Some of the clubs were always packed with half-drunk soldiers looking for a good time. I took two Land Rovers and the military police and went in search of the trouble. One particular club specialised in live entertainment. On stage was this woman. She wasn't wearing very many clothes to say the least. She stood with one leg on the ground and the other balanced on a chair and she was holding a champagne bottle. What she was doing with the champagne bottle I could hardly believe. I was standing next to the military policeman. 'Is she doing what I think she's doing with that bottle?' I asked him.

'Yes, Ma'am. No, Ma'am.' I got everyone out of there and gave them a good dressing down. No charges were made."

Pauline wasn't always in charge and occasionally enjoyed playing pranks in the Bielefield 'window shopping' streets. Here, scantily dressed girls lounged around in the window, openly inviting clients with languorous looks and fluttering eyelashes. There would be a discreet door next to the shop window with buttons indicating which lovely young lady was available for hire. "Us girls used to press button three and wait for the girl to rush to the door, expecting a client. There would, of course, be no one there."

Eventually, Pauline met a young man who was not intimidated by her powerful position, skills or personality. They began a serious relationship and married after a brief courtship. Peter Haffenden was serving with the Royal Electrical and Mechanical Engineers and must have been a soldier of some calibre and ability – but Pauline regretted her marriage. It lasted seven years and produced two sons of whom she is inordinately proud, but something in Pauline wished she had never done it. "Peer pressure had something to do with it. Everyone around us had been getting married.

Peter had been Best Man frequently, just as I had been Bridesmaid. Friends kept saying 'what about you two?' and my Mum kept asking when I was going to give her a grandchild. I was the only daughter, the only child. I can't regret my two beautiful children, nor my wonderful three granddaughters and two grandsons, but I regret the loss of my career. We brought the wedding forward when Peter learned he was going to be posted to Northern Ireland. That was a real trouble spot. My next posting would have been Hong Kong."

In those days, it wasn't thought possible to remain in the Army and stay married. Postings might separate couples, having children would be impossible. Pauline will never know how far she could have gone, but Major Maine indicated that she might well have been promoted to officer status. In one sense, that would have been difficult as Pauline always liked being one of the girls – but she was always going to be a cut above.

Her leadership was well demonstrated by her involvement in a Court Martial. Whilst in Germany, Pauline was approached by some of the army girls working on the base. They had a problem. It seemed that a Sergeant to whom they had been entrusting holiday money was reluctant to hand it over. 'We're all going home on leave next week,' they told Pauline, 'and she keeps making excuses about when she'll give it back.'

Pauline summoned a meeting in the operating room. 'All those who gave money in for safe keeping, please put your hands up.' Nearly everyone did. 'How much?' It was quite a large sum. 'Leave it to me.'

Even Pauline couldn't challenge the Sergeant herself directly, and went to find Major Maine. Pauline explained the situation: she believed the Sergeant had taken the money. She had noticed that the Sergeant had been shopping recently, acquiring a great deal of new clothes and even jewellery. 'I don't even care if you call me Cole today, Sir,' she said. 'It's a very delicate situation. I need your opinion.'

Major Maine was amused. 'That's not like you – Cole!' he said. 'You're usually very decisive. Let's go and see her.'

Major Maine asked the Sergeant to open the safe. She went pale. He made the request again, firmer. She burst into tears. The safe was empty. Not a bean. The Sergeant had taken about twelve thousand deutschmarks. She was charged with theft and Pauline attended the terrifying process of a court martial. Designed to be intimidating, the court room was panelled and formal but the occupants were grander still. Pauline had never seen so much braid, nor counted so many pips. Pauline took the stand and explained her position. She was able to give the exact amount of money missing the silly girl had given receipts.

The Sergeant was sent to a prison in Guildford. She lost her stripes, her job, and probably any chance of worthwhile employment in the future.

Major Maine paid tribute to Pauline in Court. He hoped she would stay in the army. 'You're such brilliant officer material,' he told her, 'you've come up from the ranks. They're always the best. We get the lady lieutenants coming in from Hendon – they think they know everything in five minutes.' Pauline agreed: she had her patience tested a few times by new young recruits with one pip on their shoulder.

CHAPTER SEVEN

Pauline's marriage with Peter didn't last long. It left her two adored sons, but it also left her bitter and angry. "I don't believe I ever loved him. You wouldn't think that in the space of seven years, after all I had gone through in Aden, that he could reduce me to a mental wreck. He accused me of being useless – me! According to Peter, I was a useless wife, a useless mother, I couldn't cook and I was useless in bed. I wish I'd never met him. He affected Simon, my youngest son, very badly. He winced every time Peter shouted at me. Leslie, my eldest was much stronger and wouldn't take any nonsense from his Dad. Peter joined the police force when he came out, and trained in Hendon. I consulted a solicitor – did I have grounds for divorce? Apparently, I had more than enough reason to cite mental cruelty and my divorce was granted, 10 February 1977. The judge ripped into Peter – but Simon had to see a child psychologist for the next fifteen years. It took me two years to recover."

Peter Haffenden moved to live in South Africa, remarried twice more and proceeded to fall out with all his family. Pauline, with the wisdom and perspective of years, simply feels that he was always his own worst enemy.

But although Pauline was free of Peter, she now had two small boys to bring up on her own. "I managed! I have to say that those six years in the Army, especially Aden, taught me how to cope with anything life throws at you. They made a fighter out of me – I'll fight for anything which I believe in. My training and experience kept me strong. It hasn't been easy and my health hasn't always been good, but I'll survive.

"I had to fight Peter for maintenance. I couldn't earn anything with small children. Luckily, Mum and Dad lived nearby and they helped. If you'd been in the Army, you were exempt from the normal rules of living two years in a district before you could apply for a council house. I could choose anywhere in England, Scotland or Wales. A two bedroom bungalow in Hemel Hempstead became available – near my parents. We were so poor that the boys had to share shoes: if Simon was in the pushchair, Leslie could wear them, and if Simon needed them, Leslie went barefoot."

Pauline took jobs locally, working in several shops before joining the Co-op. Inevitably, she became Manager. Leslie, tough and combative, thrived, but Simon found life much harder. The psychologist told Pauline that Simon was better, but remained troubled – that he was likely to struggle with insecurity. Worse, he found school difficult. "Dyslexia wasn't recognised so easily in those days. The school kept telling me he was stupid and lazy and I knew he wasn't. He shook whenever he had to speak to his Dad. Leslie shouted back. Leslie's like me, sporty and assertive – and Leslie's got three girls!"

Pauline's proud parents had their daughter back. "One day, Mum telephoned to say she didn't feel well. Something in her voice made me worry. I got a doctor round who listened to her heart. He told me that she had suffered a massive heart attack. He didn't know how she was still alive. She died right then, before the ambulance arrived. Pauline had to tell her father. Among much else, Pat Cole had been a championship ballroom dancer. Pauline remembers her pretty mother's wardrobes full of swirling tulle and sequins. Five long years later for her father, he met another Pat and remarried. "He used to come for lunch on Sundays with the boys. One Sunday, he explained that he was busy. I thought he might be bowling: he was a very keen player and often went on tournaments. He bowled for England with James Bryant. Rather nervously, he explained that he was courting, a word I hadn't heard for fifty years. He was worried that I might be upset, but I told him, that's nice! Army training had taught me how to handle any situation. And if I had to pick someone for Dad's second wife, I would have picked Pat. They had eighteen happy years together – and she had a daughter called Pauline.

"Once the boys were older, I could take work a little more seriously. I got a job in a nightclub! I became Bar Staff. I had a brilliant arrangement with Elaine, my neighbour who was studying. My hours were 8 p.m. to 2 a.m., and Elaine would come and work in my house whilst the boys were sleeping and I was running the Club bar. It worked for six years." Once again, Pauline found herself running the Club. "I'm an Army girl. I can sort stuff out. There were often problems with some of the girls once they'd had too much to drink. They'd pull each other's hair out. The bouncers couldn't touch them, it would be an 'assault'. I had to restrain quite a few, I can tell you."

Happiness second time round: Dad and Pat.

"I decided to run 'hen nights' and 'men nights' to bring in custom and then I started putting on drag events for charity. I wish you could have seen some of the tough bouncers dressed up...

"Then I thought I'd start my own business. I acquired two machines which covered magazines in plastic film and sealed them for posting. I called it Fulfilment. One day, I was approached by Boreham Leisure, a nationwide holiday company based in Hemel Hempstead. Would I quote for them? Of course, I would be delighted. How many did they need? Three hundred and sixty thousand. Delivered in November and out by Christmas. Ah, well, I said. Right. My ' factory' was a little shack attached to my house. I discovered a Swedish company with a 'zipman' machine that piled up the magazines one side and coughed them up, film wrapped, out of the other. All I would have to do was label them. Fine, except that it cost twenty-five thousand pounds. I didn't have twenty-five thousand pounds. But I did have a council house worth about thirty-five thousand pounds more than I'd paid for it. I went to my Bank Manager. Could you lend me the difference, I asked him. He said yes. So I had this machine imported from Sweden into my Unit and got going. I had an amazing three years.

"When I reached fifty, I decided I would retire to the seaside. I sold my company and moved here, just on the fringe of Eastbourne. I had always wanted to live by the sea in a cottage with roses round the door, and so I did. My boys were all grown up, married and producing children and I've been here now for nearly twenty years. It's been wonderful and I've had a whale of time. I've made lots of friends, we're all roughly the same age, and we have Christmas parties, Halloween parties, barbecues and pantomimes where we all forget our words and land up in hysterics. Some of the eighty years olds have more energy than I do. Kings Park is said to be the safest place in Eastbourne because everyone knows everyone else and a strange car or unexpected visitor would have all the net curtains twitching."

Typically, Pauline doesn't let the fact of ill health slow her down. She was diagnosed with diabetes and recently has almost lost her sight, but she remains upbeat and positive. A major stroke three years ago failed to quench her spirit or seriously damage her outlook on life. She was invited to become involved in Blind Veterans UK, the national charity that was St. Dunstans, near Brighton and was thrilled to receive an Invitation to the Buckingham Palace Garden Party in June this year. Pauline remains the only female blind Veteran of any armed conflict: she says she feels a bit special. She is.

Mother Amazing: Pauline recently with her boys, Simon, left, and Leslie, right.

Aden will remain the highlight of her life and now, with time for research and reflection, Pauline has started studying the history of the British involvement in the Middle East. It does not make cheerful reading: Hansard papers of the Parliamentary debates are at odds with the situation that Pauline remembers on the ground. England, far from being a country of diplomatic integrity and reliable promises, broke Treaties left right and centre, with a cavalier disregard for all interests save their own. Some of her findings follow in the next chapter: some remain to be uncovered, as papers are still 'classified' more than fifty years later. She would like to know why and has written to Cabinet officials for some answers. They may never come, an interesting fact in itself.

What seems to be clear is the dichotomy between troops on the ground, British Government officials in Aden, the Labour Government and covert operations behind the scenes. Perhaps that will never be known. The story belongs to the messy business of decolonisation which, in some countries, happened with a glorious business of swapping flags and uniforms: in Aden, there was an unceremonious scuttling and an airlifted evacuation which led to chaos seconds later. No wonder that Aden veterans never felt they were allowed to belong to commemorative parades at The Cenotaph or remembered with the same glory as survivors from Kenya, Uganda, India, Burma or Hongkong.

If Pauline Cole has anything to do with it, Aden veterans will find themselves a great deal nearer centre stage.

PAULINE COLE

Pauline recently: kind, tough and glamorous.

ADEN: THE POLITICAL BACKGROUND 1838 – 2015

1838 – The Sultan of Lahej grants seventy-five square miles of Aden and surrounding area to the British for use as a port and trading base in the area.

1839 – Royal Marines landed at Aden to protect British shipping. Aden lay between Suez, Bombay and Zanzibar, important British possessions.

1857 – Aden territory enlarged by the islands of Perim and Kuria Muria by 1900 Aden governed by president appointed by the Viceroy of India. Aden essentially run by Indians who dominated Arab/Persian tradition. Because the Indians regarded Aden as military outpost, they rejected possibilities of commercial co-operation with the Yemen and chose to extend defensive barriers between Aden and the interior by treaties of British protection to all rulers of the South Arabian coast.

1915 – Aden territories added to by the island of Kamaran.

1915 – British Empire declared war on the Ottoman Empire: Ottomans planned invasion of Aden Protectorate with local Arab tribes. Prince Feisal and T.E. Lawrence negotiate British help in Aden in return for Arab support against the Germans in WWI.

1917 – Indian Political Service relinquish control of Aden Protectorate. Aden becomes responsibility of the Foreign Office, London.

1932 – Aden created Province of India in its own right.

1937 – Aden separated from British India and transferred to Colonial Office as Crown Colony. BUT England needed forces for WW2. Impossibility of defending entire Empire in 1942 demonstrated by loss of Singapore.

1939-45 – Aden HQ for British forces Aden, primarily submarine and escort warfare. Subcommand, RAF, Middle East.

1955-56 – Beginnings of democratic elections to local governing bodies. Judicial rule entirely secular and British – no Sharia law.

1956 – Nasser nationalises Suez Canal. England joins forces with France and Israel to reclaim it: attempt fails. Suez crisis threatens world peace: dictators learn to threaten with nuclear arms. Nasser sets America against Russia. Suez no longer vital for colonial trade BUT vital to carry oil supplies and arms. UK no longer able to conduct major military intervention in the region without American backing. US refuse to intervene in Suez. Huge loss of British military and political clout: beginnings of end of colonial influence. Post Suez, Aden becomes main location in the region for the British.

1956-8 – Social unrest in Aden begins with Trade Unions set up along English lines but which do not function as English Trades Unions. Tangled skeins of economics and nationalism.

1957 – Yemeni agreements signed in Moscow and Peking. Russian arms now in use against British on Protectorate border. Russians and Chinese arrived to build ports and roads for Yemeni kingdom. Skirmishes between tribes of the Protectorate and the British took on a far more ominous character.

1958 – State of Emergency declared in Aden as increasing number of strikes threaten port and protectorate. British ignore views of local labour force which push Arabs into revolt – and into potential support for the nationalist shrieking's of Colonel Nasser.

1958 – Iraqi revolution. Hashemite monarchy, set up by the British, overthrown.

1961 – Kuwait constitutional independence. Two landmark developments towards loss of British Empire.

1963 – Colony of Aden incorporated into the Federation of Arab Emirates and renamed Federation of South Arabia. Attempt to stabilise Aden and surrounding protectorate in order to achieve eventual independence. Aden Emergency: first serious counter-insurgency against English administration.

1964 – Prime Minister Harold MacMillan: England promised independence to the FSA: no actual date then given, but proposed for 1968. Rebels redouble efforts to force English out of Aden beforehand.

1966 – British Labour Prime Minister Harold Wilson: premature announcement to leave South Arabia undermines Counter-insurgency. Nationalist groups fighting the British – and each other.

1967 – March. House of Parliament, Commons Sitting. Debate on Aden independence: Edward Heath, Leader of the Opposition, asked if Federal Leaders in Aden will reject independence if they are unable to maintain internal and external security? Issue ducked by Harold Wilson. Duncan Sandys observed that terrorist groups in Aden intend to threaten proposed United Nations visit to Aden.

1967 – March. Aden Federal Government rejected British plans for independence in November 1967. They would accept independence in September 1968 only if British forces remain to support them: if we extend a defence guarantee for up to three years and if a new constitution could be in force before September 1968. George Brown, Foreign Secretary, declared this unacceptable.

1967 – April. United Nations Mission to Aden achieved nothing and left after five days. UN expected England to remain in South Arabia for as long as required for its peace keeping to be effective.

1967 – May. A secret Memo from the Cabinet aired the question of the fate of 80,000 inhabitants of Aden and South Arabia who had Citizenship of the United Kingdom and Colonies, but no other connection with England. Action should be taken against the risk that they might seek to come to England in large numbers. An Order in Council could seek to deprive them of UK citizenship and replace that legacy with citizenship of South Arabia. This was debated in the Commons in June 1967. Jeremy Thorpe raised the question of consultation. He was shocked to learn that that residents of Perim and Kuria Muria would be involved in their future status and affiliation – but no further consultation was envisaged with the citizens of Aden.

1967 – June. Six Day War between Nasser's Egypt and Dayan's Israel. Worsening relations between Arabs and England: Arabs believed England supported Israel. Ignominious defeat for Nasser.

1967 – June. House of Parliament, Commons Sitting. Amendment tabled to delay granting independence given nationalist terrorism. BUT George Brown, Foreign Secretary, orders more troops to Aden, supplies of modern armaments and promises an aircraft carrier to cruise in the waters of South Arabia to defend the new independent Federation if necessary. This 'guarantee' of British military support for an independent FSA does not win overall support. There are convincing arguments for winning Arab support by a complete withdrawal – many MPs believed that foreign armies are a colonial remnant and do not encourage local developments nor future harmonious relationships with England.

1967 – June. Arab mutiny against British administration in Crater. Colonel Mitchell with the Argylls and Sutherland Highlanders recapture Aden, in a victorious campaign but possibly countermanding orders from Harold Wilson. June. Parliamentary debate in House of Commons over 'relinquishment of sovereignity over Aden, Perim and Kuria Muria'. Plan to delay independence discussed.

1967 – July. Debate in the House of Lords; declaration of policy to grant independence to Aden, Kuria Muria and Perim on 9 January 1968. Lords Jellicoe and Shackleton expressed admiration for the skill and efficiency displayed by British troops for the re-occupation of Crater: they admired the minimum of casualties and praised 'a remarkable operation'. Both asked if the Commanders (no names) had discretion over weapons, an issue aired by some controversial statements in the newspapers. (They did: the UK press were wrong.) Lord Jellicoe observed Shackleton's missions to Aden which presume – although not specified in The House – a certain consultation process. Jellicoe explained that 'normally independence comes after full consultation with the peoples involved after a Constitution has been agreed and on the principle of majority rule. But there had been no free elections for two years'. Terrorism had frozen democracy. Shackleton confirmed an earlier Treaty to keep Aden within the Federation of South Arabia until 1969. Lord Gladwyn, Deputy Leader of the Lords, put the matter in context. He explained that in 1965, his Party was the first to advocate an early withdrawal by England from her various bases in the Persian Gulf and still felt this was desirable WITHIN a co-ordinated scheme involving Singapore, Australia and South East Asia. He believed that there was no point in evacuating Aden and hanging indefinitely on elsewhere in the Persian Gulf, viz, Bahrein. He did not think UK bases were consonant with the rising tide of Arab nationalism. Our oil interests would have to be protected by diplomacy, not military might. Gladwyn aired an earlier question of self-governance for Aden: this would enable Aden to determine its own future. Wise words: too late. Independence, also discussed, was dismissed as playing into the hands of Nasser.

Long debates in both Houses during late June/early July 1967, aired our history and responsibility to the Arab people of Aden. Lady Kinloss explained that the land was so barren, rocky and lacked most natural resources that only 2% could be cultivated. There was no oil. Education and medicine depended upon outside support for funds and trained staff. Lord Segal felt it was the duty of the Moslem nations to support fellow Moslems, and not the British: and if they seemed reluctant, they should be ordered to by the United Nations. It was generally felt that the UN should take charge, an idea entertainingly welcomed by George Brown who had presumed that Conservatives customarily failed to offer the UN sufficient support.

1967 – Continuing deadly attacks against British forces in Aden make Harold Wilson decide to evacuate base in November 1967, earlier than planned and WITH NO agreement on succeeding governance. British leave, with covert assistance from NLF. December, NLF seize power in Aden. Loss of British support for the oil-poor Yemenis: difficulty of obtaining valuable business and revenue severely disrupts economic growth for years.

1969 – Radical Marxist wing of NLF seize power. Reorganised country into People's Democratic Republic of Yemen. Subsequently, all political parties amalgamated into National Liberation Front, then renamed Yemeni Socialist Party which became the only legal party.

1986 – Violent struggle in Aden between supporters of rival factions of the PDRY: South Yemen Civil War broke out with thousands of casualties.

Late 1980s – Against background of Perestroika, the USSR, Yemen's main backer, South Yemen started political reforms.

1990 – Parties reached full agreement on joint governance of Yemen and countries eventually merged as Yemen. Aden, country and port, declared a Free Trade zone.

2015 – Breaking news: Saudi-led coalition forces range against new religious fundamentalist group, the 'Houthis' or Believers in God. Aden in front line for armed conflict between Yemenis and Saudis against fanatical fundamentalists.

Hansard, Philip Goodhart, MP, Beckenham.

Printed in Great Britain
by Amazon